A McGRAW-HILL NATURAL SCIENCE PICTURE BOOK

Scientific Adviser : Dr. Gwynne Vevers
Curator of the Aquarium, The Zoological Society of London

Animal Life in the Antarctic

F. D. OMMANNEY

ILLUSTRATED BY

ROBERT GILLMOR

McGRAW-HILL BOOK COMPANY

NEW YORK · ST. LOUIS · SAN FRANCISCO

MCGRAW-HILL NATURAL SCIENCE PICTURE BOOKS

ANIMALS OF THE ARCTIC by Dr. Gwynne Vevers
Curator of the Aquarium, The Zoological Society of London

ANIMALS OF THE DESERT by J. L. Cloudsley-Thompson

ANTS AND TERMITES by Dr. Gwynne Vevers

APES AND MONKEYS by Dr. Desmond Morris

BATS by Dr. David Pye

THE BIG CATS by Dr. Desmond Morris

THE CURIOUS WORLD OF SNAKES by Alfred Leutscher
Co-founder and first Secretary, British Herpetological Society

LIFE IN THE SEA by Dr. Gwynne Vevers

ELEPHANTS AND MAMMOTHS by Dr. Gwynne Vevers

THE ORIGINS OF MAN by Dr. John Napier
Director of Primate Biology Program, Smithsonian Institution, Washington, D.C.

PLANTS THAT EAT ANIMALS by Dr. Linna Bentley
Lecturer in Botony, Bedford College, University of London

THE SMALL WATER MAMMALS by Maxwell Knight

THE STARS by Colin A. Ronan

ANIMAL LIFE IN THE ANTARCTIC

First distribution in the United States of America by
McGraw-Hill Book Company, 1971

Contents

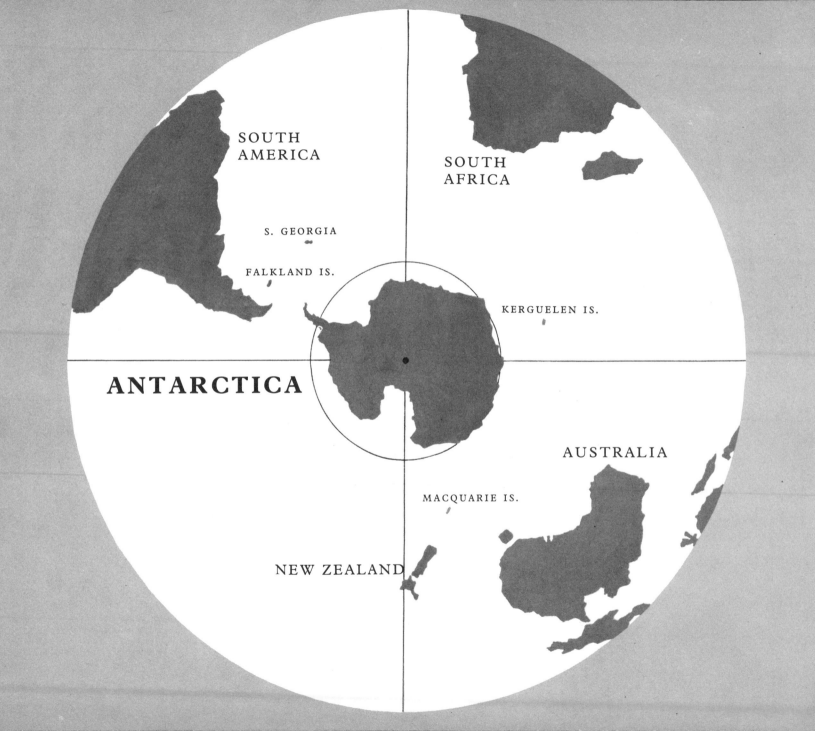

The Antarctic

The Antarctic zone strictly comprises all the land, islands and sea within the Antarctic circle, which is drawn along latitude $66\frac{1}{2}°$ South, just as the Arctic circle is drawn along latitude $66\frac{1}{2}°$ North. As far as living things are concerned, however, the boundary lies farther north and includes the island of South Georgia and the Kerguelen group.

The Antarctic continent itself supports almost no life at all—no human beings or four-footed creatures. Myriads of sea birds and seals live on the cliff faces and the shores but they owe their existence to the sea, which is also the home of the great whales. Whales feed in Antarctic seas during the southern summer (November to April) but go north to breed in tropical waters during the winter (May to October). Many birds and all seals inhabit Antarctic seas all the year round.

Whalebone whales

Whales are of two kinds: those with teeth in their mouths and those with no teeth but horny plates of whalebone hanging in close-set series from each upper jaw, their inner edges frayed out to form a mat of coarse hairs. In Antarctic seas these whalebone whales feed entirely on swarms of small animals, called krill, that somewhat resemble shrimps. They engulf them in their mouths and sieve them out of the water through the hairs on the whalebone plates. Whales are shaped like fish but are in fact mammals. They live entirely at sea but breathe air into lungs and blow up a spout of water vapor when they exhale. They swim about the ocean in "schools" and bear and nurse their young just as other mammals do but in the open ocean. Instead of having a furry coat the whale is protected from the cold by a layer of fat under the skin called the blubber. The forked tail beats up and down and not sideways like that of a fish, and the forefins retain the bones of five fingers bound together by skin and gristle. The rear limbs, however, have quite disappeared.

The whalebone whales are the largest animals on earth, and a cow blue whale may reach a length of 100 feet, though none as large as this are to be seen nowadays. Bulls are slightly smaller than cows. Another kind of whalebone whale common in Antarctic seas is the fin whale or finback which is somewhat smaller than the blue.

Two fin whales and a blue whale ►

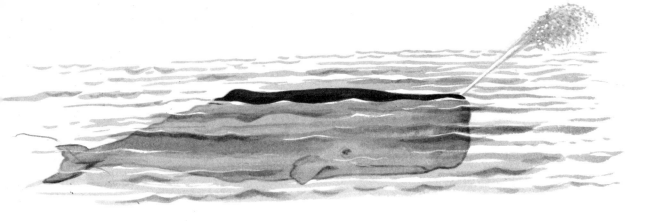

The sperm whale or cachalot

This is the largest of the whales with teeth, all of which are meat-eaters. Underneath its barrel-shaped head is a slitlike mouth and a lower jaw like a rod armed on each side with a row of strong conical teeth. This is used for seizing the squids on which the whale feeds, for snapping rather than chewing. The upper jaw has only traces of teeth. Inside the head is a reservoir, actually a buoyancy tank to help it float correctly, containing a waxy oil called spermaceti which was at one time used for making candles.

The squids on which the sperm whale feeds have horny beaks in their heads which are indigestible. They set up an irritation in the whale's intestine which gives off a slimy mucus around them and then voids the whole lump into the sea. These lumps, when found cast up on beaches, are known as ambergris and were once much valued for use in making perfume.

Sperm whales are really tropical animals and travel about in smaller schools or larger herds. In Antarctic waters only big solitary bulls are found which, for some unknown reason, have left the main herds in the tropics.

A large bull sperm whale may reach 60 feet, but the cows are never more than half that length.

The killer whale or grampus

This is another toothed whale and one of the fiercest and most ruthless hunters of the sea. It feeds on whales, seals, penguins, and other birds. When attacking whales or seals, it tears lumps out of the back with its powerful teeth which are in both jaws. Smaller prey, such as birds, it seizes and swallows whole. Explorers have described how killer whales have been seen to prowl around ice floes on which men were standing as though waiting to seize them if they fell into the water, and have even bumped the floes with their backs as though to dislodge the men on them.

The killer whale has a large, triangular back fin which makes it unmistakable at a distance. In old bulls this becomes very large indeed and occupies about a fifth of the length of the body.

Killers are found in all the seas of the world but are most abundant in Arctic and Antarctic waters.

Killer whales chasing Weddell seals ►

Seals

The only mammals in the Antarctic other than whales are the seals. They, too, have a streamlined shape because they live in water, but they still have their hind limbs. There are two kinds of seals in the Antarctic: fur seals and true seals. Fur seals have ears visible on the outside of the head and can turn their hind limbs forward so as to use them for hobbling, often quite rapidly, on land. True seals have no visible ears and use their hind limbs only for swimming. They are almost helpless when out of water and can only flop along on their bellies with feeble help from their forelimbs. Yet they haul themselves out of the sea onto beaches, or onto ice floes, for breeding, to molt their coats, or to sleep. Here are four true seals. The leopard seal (above), so named from the dark spots on its back, is a lithe, slender animal about 10 feet long, with a strong head and formidable snapping jaws. It feeds mainly on penguins which it pursues with great agility and speed under water.

The crabeater or white seal (above) is about 8 feet long. It lies on ice floes, often hundreds of miles from land, and bears its pups there in the early spring. Despite its name it does not eat crabs but feeds entirely on krill and other small shrimplike creatures which it filters from the water with its teeth.

The Weddell seal (right, with pup), named after Captain James Weddell, an English sealer, is the most southerly of Antarctic mammals, frequenting the coasts of the continent itself and outlying islands. It is about the same length as the crabeater, less slender than the leopard, and is quite helpless out of water since its foreflippers do not touch the ground, so that it can only wriggle along on its belly. When disturbed it makes a little piping noise and, if provoked, opens its mouth and hisses. It feeds on squids and krill.

The Ross seal (below), named after Sir James Clark Ross who first sighted the Great Ross barrier, has pouches in its neck around the windpipe which help to produce a loud trumpeting cry. It, too, leads a solitary life in the pack ice and is never seen outside the Antarctic circle.

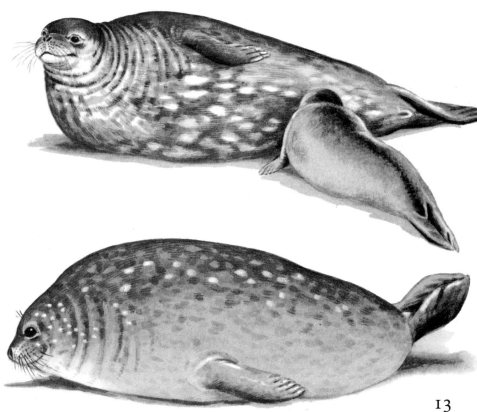

The elephant seal or sea elephant

This is the largest of the true seals in the Antarctic. It breeds mainly on northerly islands such as South Georgia and Macquarie Island and is not found south of the Antarctic circle. It has a layer of thick blubber under its skin which produces an oil as good as whale oil.

The bull grows to a length of about 20 feet and the cow about half that size. The bull has a protuberance on his nose which he inflates when angry, and it is the fancied resemblance of this to an elephant's trunk that gives the seal its name.

Elephant seals come up onto the beaches in the spring to mate and bear their young. The cows are grouped in "harems", each in the charge of a bull, and the bulls fight together for the cows, rearing up on their hind ends, inflating their noses, and roaring. They lunge forward repeatedly onto one another and often inflict severe wounds. The pups from last year's mating are born in the early spring, and the cows call to them with a whining sound. After the birth of the pups, mating takes place. As the black woolly pups feed from their mothers the warmth of their bodies melts deep holes in the snow in which the cows and their pups lie as though entombed. Later on the "rookery", as the colony is called, becomes a quagmire of mud, and the noise from it can be heard a long way off. At midsummer the harems break up, and the seals put to sea to feed on squids. In the autumn they return to the beaches to molt and sleep, but they are no longer in harems and the bulls lie apart from the cows, taking no notice of them at all. With the onset of winter they all go to sea again, not to return until the spring.

The fur seal

The fur seal has only a thin layer of blubber under the skin, but instead has a very thick furry coat. Both the bull and the cow have a mane, but the bull's is especially thick and forms a crest or "wig" of erect hairs on top of his head.

The fur seal has greatly increased in numbers in recent years on some Antarctic islands, mostly to the northward, and the best known colonies are on an island off the northernmost tip of South Georgia.

The bulls come ashore into rocky coves in the spring and establish territories for themselves, fighting furiously for ownership. Later the cows arrive to bear their pups, and the bulls claim those which come ashore in their territories, grouping them into harems. A black woolly pup is born to each cow a few days after she arrives. Mating then takes place, after which the cows make trips to sea to feed on krill, leaving their pups on the beaches where they collect in groups or "pods" and spend the time during their mothers' absence sleeping, playing, and mock fighting. As each cow returns from a feeding trip she howls to her pup and can recognize it among hundreds of others. She then takes it up to the back of the beach and feeds it.

In late summer the harems begin to break up and the seals molt. Fur seals do not lie on the beaches to do this but shed hair both on shore and in the sea. The pups now acquire a coat of beautiful silver gray fur. The bulls, who have not fed at all since they came ashore in the spring, are by now very thin, and all the seals take to the sea for the winter.

Penguins

Penguins, though almost entirely confined to the southern hemisphere, are not peculiar to the Antarctic and some do not live there at all. Three kinds—the Adélie, the ringed, and the emperor—live and breed on the Antarctic continent.

All penguins, although they are birds, have lost the power of flight, and their wings have become flippers with which they swim rapidly under water. Their bodies are streamlined and their feathers are like scales, lubricated with oil from the skin so as to slip easily through the water. Like whales and seals they have an insulating layer of fat under the skin. In the Antarctic, they feed on krill and other shrimplike creatures, often far out at sea.

The Adélie penguin (above) is the commonest and most numerous of the truly Antarctic penguins. It stands about $2\frac{1}{2}$ feet high and congregates in vast rookeries, usually on low rocky ground near the sea. Out at sea, often far from land, Adélie penguins rest on ice floes and icebergs.

The Adélies gather in their rookeries in the early spring and go through an elaborate courtship, bowing and chortling, the cocks (the males) picking up stones in their beaks to lay them at the feet of possible mates.

The hen makes a nest of stones roughly arranged in a ring and lays two eggs in it. The chicks hatch out in about five weeks, covered with gray down. Both parents look after the eggs and chicks, taking turns to go to sea to find food.

The chicks feed by placing their heads inside the open beak of the parent who disgorges part of the food contents of the crop, a pouch in the bird's throat. When the chicks are nearly as large as their parents they are herded together in groups of ten or twenty called "nurseries", while the parents go away to sea to feed. The parents repeatedly return to feed their young but, with the approach of autumn, cease to recognize them and yield only to the cries of the nearest and most insistent of the young. Later the parents stop feeding the young altogether. When the ice and snow return the rookeries disperse and both old and young, now in full adult plumage, go to sea for the winter.

The ringed or chinstrap penguin

This is the commonest and most numerous penguin in the sector of the Antarctic south of South America. It is about the same size as the Adélie and much like it in general habits and breeding cycle. It chooses steeper and more inaccessible places for its nests, often on cliff faces hundreds of feet above the sea, and often hops onto steep icebergs which the Adélies would not attempt. It is a much fiercer, braver bird than the Adélie and will repeatedly return to attack an intruder after being repulsed. It vigorously chases away birds of prey from its nest until parental care in due course begins to relax.

As the summer goes on the whole area of a rookery becomes a trampled mass of droppings. The smell is overpowering and the chattering and quarrelling never cease. Penguins spend a lot of time in what looks like gossip and will go for any intruder with blind fury, pecking and slapping with their flippers. Birds of prey (skua gulls, giant petrels, and "paddies") continually haunt the rookeries, seizing and devouring the eggs and chicks.

Chinstrap penguin in ecstatic display

21

The emperor penguin

The emperor is the largest of the penguins, standing about 4 feet high. It breeds on the coast of the continent in midwinter and forms its rookeries on the permanent sea ice close inshore. The birds come onto the ice in March or early April and go through an elaborate courtship, bowing with their necks swollen out and rubbing their beaks against their flippers. They group themselves together in compact clusters or "huddles" of ten to thirty birds until mating when the hen falls flat on her white waistcoat, or is pushed over by her mate. He mounts her with difficulty because numerous disengaged males rush to do the same so that he has to fight to beat off his rivals. He does not always succeed. No nest is made and in June, which is midwinter in the Antarctic, the hen lays a single large egg, holding it on the upper surfaces of her feet covered by a fold of the skin of her belly. However, the day after laying it she parts her feet and lets it roll on to the ice. The cock then picks it up on the backs of his feet and covers it with a similar fold of skin. The egg is then hatched by the male while the female goes away to sea. During incubation the males all group themselves together in one enormous huddle of several thousand birds and so store up body heat. The chicks, with gray down and white goggles, hatch out in seven or eight weeks. The instant a chick appears it is set upon by eager males who have either never found a mate or lost their egg, and they fight furiously with each other for the chick. The chick itself may be torn to pieces or trampled to death, but a deprived and eggless male may nurse the tiny frozen corpse until the down is quite worn off it. After the chicks hatch out, the well-fed females return and take charge of their offspring while their thin, shabby husbands in turn leave the rookery. In September the chicks are grouped in nurseries and are fed by both males and females who, however, no longer recognize their own children. By early January the rookeries have dispersed.

Other penguins

A few other penguins may be regarded as Antarctic though they breed mainly on northerly islands.

The gentoo penguin (left) makes its rookeries near the sea, the nests usually sheltered by a rock or a bunch of coarse grass. The hen takes some care in making her nest, neatly arranging a circle of stones, bits of grass, and moss brought to her by her mate. Two eggs are laid, one a few days after the other, so that the chicks are of different sizes. Gentoo rookeries do not get into quite such a filthy state as those of Adélie or ringed penguins, and the chick is better cared for. The gentoo is rather a timid bird and, at the approach of an

intruder, usually deserts its nest temporarily. Gentoo eggs are excellent to eat though they have a deep red yolk.

The king penguin (above, opposite) is the handsomest of all. It is a relation of the emperor but smaller (2½–3 feet) and, like the emperor, makes no nest but carries the single egg on the upper surfaces of its feet covered by a fold of skin.

Macaroni, the old term for an overdressed gentleman, also describes the macaroni penguin (above, left). These penguins form large rookeries on slopes covered with tussock grass. The macaroni is a fierce, quarrelsome bird and its rookeries are perhaps the smelliest of all with a pungent goatlike smell.

The rock-hopper penguin (above, right) is a small cousin of the macaroni and lives on Heard Island and the Kerguelen group.

The wandering albatross

More than half the other sea birds which live in the Antarctic regions are petrels, that is, they have the nostrils continued along the beak as a pair of tubes nearly as far as the tip. Some, like the wandering albatross and the giant petrel, are huge birds, while others, such as Wilson's storm petrel, are very small, not much larger than a horned lark. Most of the petrels breed on northerly islands.

The most beautiful and famous of the petrels is the wandering albatross which is often seen at sea soaring on motionless wings with a span of as much as 14 feet. Though majestic in the air, it is ungainly on land and nests on the tussock-covered slopes of South Georgia and Kerguelen Islands.

Wanderers come on land in December and perform their courtship dance which lasts for days. The nests are conical mounds of mud and grass dotted about the slopes, always overlooking a steep face so that the birds can get a good take-off, for they cannot rise into the air from the level. The cock collects the material for the nest and brings it to his mate who arranges it with her beak, and the pair show great affection for one another, constantly interrupting their work to dance and clap their beaks.

On or near Christmas Day the hen lays her large single egg, white with red markings and containing three-quarters of a pint of liquid. These great birds are quite unafraid of human beings and the egg can be taken away from the nest while the hen is still sitting on it. She does not budge but only mildly claps her beak in protest.

The chick, hatched in February or March, looks in its fluffy white down like a large powder puff. Both parents sit on it in turns for the first six weeks after which it becomes too big, and both parents go away to sea in search of food—krill and similar shrimp-like animals—leaving the chick sitting on the nest alone, except for its hundreds of neighbors.

It sits thus for ten months, throughout the whole of the following winter, while both parents feed it, bringing up the contents of their crops which the chick greedily devours from the parent's beak. It is still there the following Christmas but by then it is clothed in yellowish down and looks larger than its parents. Soon after Christmas it molts and leaves the nest.

Since the parent birds have not got rid of their last year's chick by the time the next breeding season is due to begin, the wandering albatross does not breed every year, but probably in alternate years.

The giant petrel

A few petrels live and breed south of the Antarctic circle. The largest is the giant petrel or "stinker"—so-called because, if approached on shore or on the nest, it opens its beak and shoots forth the foul-smelling contents of its stomach. It is a large, ugly, ungainly bird, nearly as big as an albatross, with a similar gliding flight. On land it is very awkward and waddles slowly about with legs bent and wings outstretched, an undignified gait which has earned it the nickname "Nelly". The "stinker" cannot get into the air from a level land based take-off. On the water it must run along the surface against the wind, flapping its wings, until it has gained enough momentum to launch itself into the air. From a beach it has to take to the sea before it can take off. "Stinkers" often gorge themselves until they become too heavy to fly and must then either wait until they have digested some of the food or lighten themselves by vomiting into the water. Their natural diet consists of penguin chicks or any dead animals they can find. "Stinkers" breed all over the Antarctic and their nests, mounds of moss and stones, are built facing the sea where there is a good take-off. One egg is laid and the chick that hatches from it is clothed in grayish down. Both parents feed it by bringing up the contents of their crops, but the chick does not winter on the nest and leaves at the end of summer.

Other petrels

The Cape pigeon (above, left) is one of the most familiar birds in the Antarctic, swarming in thousands around whaling stations to feed on scraps, though its natural food consists of small marine animals. It is not a pigeon, although it looks rather like one. It nests on high cliffs on southerly islands and on the continent itself.

The beautiful silver gray fulmar petrel (above, right) is very similar to the Cape pigeon in habits but is not often seen as far north as South Georgia. It often nests among colonies of Cape pigeons and associates with them when feeding, stealing their food by force.

SNOW PETREL   ANTARCTIC PETREL   PRION   WILSON'S PETREL

The snow petrel and Antarctic petrel are inhabitants of the pack ice, and their appearance round a ship always means that the pack ice is not far off.

The whale bird or prion is only seen out at sea for it never comes within ten miles of land during daylight. At sea flocks of whale birds are a common sight, wheeling and turning together low over the water. They nest in burrows on high mountainsides all over the Antarctic but only approach and leave them at dusk because they and their chicks are preyed upon by the fierce skua gull.

The smallest of the petrels is Wilson's storm petrel. It rides on the surface of the waves and flutters above the water like a large moth, but on land it can scarcely walk.

Other birds

Two sorts of gulls live on Antarctic coasts: the black-backed Dominican gull (top, left) and the brown skua (middle, left), the fiercest bird of prey in the Antarctic. It breeds all over the region, making nests on open ground on the crests of hillocks, and preys ruthlessly on penguin and whale bird chicks and eggs.

The wreathed tern (top, right), with a black cap on its head, is the only bird which lives and breeds all over the Antarctic. It nests in colonies on high open ground. When a "ternery" is approached, all the birds rise into the air screaming shrilly and diving down at the visitor's head.

A cormorant, known as the blue-eyed or king shag (bottom, left), breeds on most Antarctic islands, feeding on fish which it catches by diving, like all cormorants. Its peculiarity is that it has china-blue eyes.

31

The sheathbill or "paddy" is the only truly land bird in the Antarctic and does not have webbed feet. It has a horny sheath at the base of the upper part of the beak and its plumage is snow white. It has a quick fussy walk, bobbing its head like a pigeon, and the curious habit of perching on rocks quite motionless for several minutes. It then flies or runs hurriedly to another place and perches again. "Paddies" frequent beaches and penguin rookeries, stealing and devouring the eggs and chicks. They eat practically anything, including shellfish, seaweed and dead animals. They nest in holes and crannies among the rocks.